Making Choices at HOME

By Diane Lindsey Reeves

21st Century Junior Library

Published in the United States of America by
Cherry Lake Publishing
Ann Arbor, Michigan
www.cherrylakepublishing.com

Reading Adviser: Marla Conn MS. Ed., Literacy specialist, Read-Ability, Inc.

Photo Credits: Cover, © Zurijeta; page 4, © kwanchai.c; page 6, © Tom Burlison; page 8, © bbernard; page 10, © Monkey Business Images; page 12, © Monkey Business Images; page 14, © Monkey Business Images; page 16, © Iakov Filimonov; page 18, © Rawpixel.com; page 20, d13. *Source: Shutterstock.*

Library of Congress Cataloging-in-Publication Data
Names: Reeves, Diane Lindsey, 1959- author.
Title: Making choices at home / by Diane Lindsey Reeves.
Description: Ann Arbor : Cherry Lake Publishing, [2018] | Series: Smart choices | Audience: K to Grade 3. | Includes bibliographical references and index.
Identifiers: LCCN 2017033738 | ISBN 9781534107861 (hardcover) | ISBN 9781534109841 (pdf) | ISBN 9781534108851 (pbk.) | ISBN 9781534120839 (hosted ebook)
Subjects: LCSH: Choice (Psychology)–Juvenile literature. | Decision making–Juvenile literature.
Classification: LCC BF611 .R44 2018 | DDC 153.8/3--dc23
LC record available at https://lccn.loc.gov/2017033738

Cherry Lake Publishing would like to acknowledge the work of The Partnership for 21st Century Skills. Please visit *www.p21.org* for more information.

Printed in the United States of America.

CONTENTS

Wake up, sleepyhead! It's time to get up.

In the Morning

Goodbye, cozy bed. Hello, new day.

You have to get up. Will you do it quickly? Or will you take so long your mom gets mad?

What kind of **attitude** will you have today? Will you be nice? Or will you be difficult?

Think about your answers as you make up your bed! You have choices to make. What will they be?

My Choice!

- Be cheerful
- Be grumpy

They both taste good. Which one is good for you?

Hungry? It's time for breakfast! Food gives you the **energy** to go, go, go.

Will you make healthy choices? Eat **grains**, **proteins**, fruits, vegetables, and dairy. These will fill you right up.

Sugary snacks taste really good. But they aren't good for you.

Eat for fun? Or eat for **fuel**? It's your choice.

My Choice!

- Eat healthy foods
- Eat unhealthy foods

Good **grooming** helps you look your best.

Take a look in the mirror. Yikes! You are still in your pajamas. Your hair is a mess. You can't go to school looking like that.

Will you jump in the shower? Or wash up at the sink? Brush teeth or hair first?

Do you grab dirty clothes off the floor? Or look for a fresh outfit in the closet? Don't forget clean underwear and socks!

You have choices to make. Ready, set, go!

My Choice!

- Look my best
- Look messy

Ready to roll? It's time for school.

Hurry up! It's time to leave! Mornings can go one of two ways.

One way is smooth. You made a smart plan. Everything you need is ready to go.

The other way is bumpy. You rush to fill your backpack and get out the door.

One choice makes mornings easy. The other brings **stress**. It's time to get going. The choices are yours.

My Choice!

- Plan ahead
- Wait until the last minute

School is over. It's time to go home.

After School

School is out. You are ready for fun!

What are your favorite things to do after school? Play sports or make music? Goof off outside? Play games or watch TV?

There are so many choices. Do a little of this. Then a little of that. You don't have to pick just one!

My Choice!

- Try lots of new activities
- Only watch TV and play video games

Finish homework or play first?

Do you have homework? You can do it as soon as you get home. Or you can work on it later. Your parents can help you choose the best plan.

You can get mad about having to do homework. But it won't get the job done.

Or you can decide homework is important to do. Take pride in your work. Ask for help when you need it.

My Choice!

- Do homework first before you forget
- Play first and do homework later

Chores are easier when everyone pitches in.

Every family has **chores**. Everyone who lives in the house helps take care of the chores. It is only fair!

How can you help your family today? Can you clean your room? Set the table? Feed the pets? Gather trash?

Being helpful says "I love you" to your parents. Sometimes it's even better than hugs!

My Choice!

- Do my part
- Let others do all the work

Chilling out with siblings is a nice way to end the day.

Do you have brothers or sisters? If so, lucky you! Having **siblings** can be fun. There is always someone to talk to and play with.

How do you treat your siblings? With kindness and respect? Or do you pick on them and fuss about sharing?

It might be hard to do this. But be kind to your siblings. They will be kind back to you.

My Choice!

- Get along with my siblings
- **Argue** with my siblings

Just one more story. Then it's time for bed.

Time for Bed

Another busy day comes to an end. Do you have a bedtime **routine**? Maybe Mom sings you a song. Maybe Dad reads your favorite book to you.

Think about the choices you made today. Celebrate the good ones that you made!

My Choice!

- I am happy about all the good choices I made
- I need to make better choices tomorrow

MY SMART CHOICES

Write a story about two different days. One day you make smart choices at home. The other day you don't. How are the two days different? Which day did you enjoy the most?

GLOSSARY

argue (AHR-gyoo) to disagree about something

attitude (AT-ih-tood) ideas and feelings that affect how you behave

chores (CHORZ) jobs that must be done around the house

energy (EN-ur-jee) the ability or strength to do things without getting tired

fuel (FYOO-uhl) something, like good food, that gives you energy

grains (GRAYNZ) foods made from crops such as wheat, corn, rice, oats, and barley

grooming (GROOM-ing) things you do to make your appearance clean and neat

proteins (PROH-teenz) foods such as meat, cheese, eggs, beans, and fish

routine (roo-TEEN) a regular way of doing things

sibling (SIB-ling) a brother or sister

stress (STRES) worry caused by problems

INDEX

ABOUT THE AUTHOR

When Diane Lindsey Reeves isn't writing children's books, she chooses to play with her four grandchildren. She lives in Cary, North Carolina and Washington, D.C.